CONTENTS

Fun at the seaside   4

Fun in the sand   6

Be safe   8

Fun in the sea   10

Time for lunch   12

Sea shells   14

Rock pools   16

It's windy!   18

Time for ice-cream   20

Glossary   22

Index   24

Words in **bold** are explained in the glossary.

Fun at the seaside

We are going to the seaside.

Don't forget to put on **sun screen**.

5

Fun in the sand

You can build a sandcastle.

Sandcastle

6

Look! A sand car.

Be safe

The **green flag** tells you it is safe to swim.

8

You must tell a grown-up
when you go into the water.

9

Fun in the sea

We love to go in the sea.

It's fun to splash!

Time for lunch

You can have a **picnic**.

Apple

Sandwich

Orange juice

13

Sea shells

We look for **sea shells**.

Smooth

Spiky

Shiny

15

Rock pools

We look in **rock pools**.

Shell

16

Crab

Starfish

Seaweed

17

It's windy!

We fly a kite!

The wind blows the kite.

Kite

19

Time for ice-cream

You can buy an ice-cream.

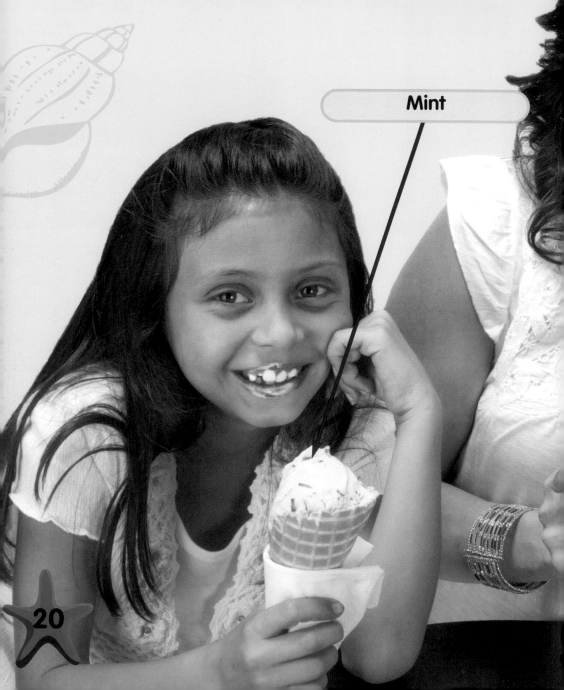

Mint

Vanilla

Strawberry

21

Glossary

green flag
This is a sign to show that a beach is safe for swimming.

picnic
A meal, such as lunch, which you eat outside.

rock pool

A small pool of seawater on a beach. The sea covers the pool for some of each day.

sea shell

The outside part of a sea animal.

sun screen

A cream that protects your skin from the sun.

23

Index

crabs 17

green flag 8, 22

ice-cream 20–21

kites 18–19

picnics 12–13, 22

rock pools 16–17, 23

safety 8–9

sandcastles 6–7

sea 10–11

sea shells 14–15, 16, 23

seaweed 17

starfish 6–7

sun screen 5, 23

Publisher: Melissa Fairley
Art Director: Faith Booker
Editor: Emma Dods
Designer: Sara Greasley
Production Controller: Ed Green
Production Manager: Suzy Kelly

ISBN: 978 1 84898 233 8

Picture credits (t=top, b=bottom, c=centre, l=left, r=right, OFC=outside front cover, OBC=outside back cover):
Image Source Black/Alamy: 5, 7. iStock: 4, 8, 10–11, 18–19, 22tl. Sharon Montrose/Getty Images: 12, 22b.
Shutterstock: OFC, Flap, 1, 2, 7t, 13 (all), 15 (all), 17 (all), 20–21, 23cr, 23b, OBC.
Adrian Weinbrecht/Getty Images: 16, 23t.

Every effort has been made to trace the copyright holders, and we apologize in advance for any unintentional omissions.
We would be pleased to insert the appropriate acknowledgements in any subsequent edition of this publication.

24